The Cornish Dancer

By the same author

Poems
History of Him
Twists of the Way
The Fiesta
Angles and Circles
Sad Grave of an Imperial Mongoose
Penguin Modern Poets 23 (with Edwin Muir and Adrian Stokes)
Discoveries of Bones and Stones
Ingestion of Ice Cream
A Skull in Salop
Collected Poems
The Isles of Scilly
Under the Cliff
Several Observations

Celebration and Criticism
The Goddess of Loving
Britain Observed
The Englishman's Flora
Notes from an Odd Country
The Contrary View
Poems and Poets

Anthologies
The Oxford Book of Satirical Verse
Rainbows, Fleas and Flowers
The Faber Book of Poems and Places
The Faber Book of Love Poems
The Faber Book of Popular Verse
The Faber Book of Nonsense Verse
The Penguin Book of Ballads
Unrespectable Verse

The Cornish Dancer
and Other Poems

Geoffrey Grigson

Secker & Warburg
London

First published in England 1982 by
Martin Secker & Warburg Limited
54 Poland Street, London W1V 3DF

Copyright © Geoffrey Grigson 1982

British Library Cataloguing in Publication Data

Grigson, Geoffrey
  The Cornish dancer and other poems.
  I. Title
  821'.912   PR6013.R744

ISBN 0-436-18805-8

Printed in Great Britain by
Redwood Burn Limited
Trowbridge

For H. M. J. G.

Whatever waits to be born,
Let's retain sentiments of the dawn,
And — somewhere — scarlet in corn.

Acknowledgements

Poems in this collection have appeared first in *Encounter*, *The Listener*, the *London Magazine*, the *New Statesman*, *Quarto* and *The Times Literary Supplement*

Contents

Abandoned Village	9
Blue Shell	10
Do You See Your Feet?	11
After a Biography	12
After a Death, Agreed	12
Châteaubriand on Le Grand Bey	13
Jeux Sans Frontières	14
History is Changed	15
Six Poems from Christian Morgenstern	16
i The Funnels	16
ii Philosophy is Born	16
iii Korf's Clock	17
iv The Moonsheep	17
v The Salmon	18
vi On the Planet of Flies	19
Foreign Travel	20
In Exile	22
The Return	23
Cluck and Crow	24
Outside His Verandah	25
Night with Mist	26
Again and Again	27
No Trouble	28
Heart Failure	29
Ruskin's View, Kirby Lonsdale	30
Sick Priest	31
Cleric on the Air	32
A Broken Wheel	33
Idyll in a Victorian Vicarage	34
A Visit to the Ledger Stones of Clerical Ancestors	35
S.F.	36
Smooth Accident	37
Return to England	38
A Relic	39
Over the Hills	40
The Pairs	41
How Is It?	42
Chicory-Eyed Author	43
Without Regret	44

45	Four Poems about Poetry
45	*i Poetry*
45	*ii The Difficult Poems*
45	*iii Transference*
45	*iv The Offering*
46	Advice to a Half-Hatched Poet
47	Sentimental Error Among Ruins
47	With It
48	The Floods
49	Water-Mill of Love
49	Antic
50	Atavists
51	Drunken Drivers See the Sights at Whitsun
52	Satellite
53	Battlefield
54	Swans and Beetles
55	The Widow
55	Dubious Marriage
56	The Wicked Poet
57	The Cornish Dancer
58	Saint in the Summer Rain
59	A Vision
59	Thank You
60	If I Could Suppose
61	Sedum acre *Linn.*
62	Shaving
62	Emeritus
62	New Year's Eve
63	Become Old
63	On a Sentimental Charlatan
63	At the Lectern
64	The Fresh One
64	Tolling the Same
64	All Square

Abandoned Village

After a thousand years this village dies:
A cough sounds from a last inhabitant
Through a shuttered door. Below, cliffs
Of a gorge. In clefts, only a loose-stone path
Goes down, above rapids, pools and falls. So,
A last man-life dies.

Rats left long ago. Swallows ceased coming. No
Swifts scythe screaming in, under stone tiles.
High nettles cross still sooted oven mouths.
Nothing crows, bleats, mews, barks, lows. Only
Coughing again, behind that bolted door, as
A last man-life dies.

Between crags in shadow and sunlight higher,
A slow eagle family soars. These eagles
Catch a lift of air, these eagles have nothing
At all to fear. By other living life
Is reassured, though this last man-life
Coughs up and dies.

Down here pennywort flattens to lizard
Walls and water-boatmen skate a black
Polished pool, from which a trickle slides.
"So be it." Coughing comes feebler from behind
These unplastered, brown, wind-bitten walls, as
This last man-life dies.

Blue Shell

To have been a blue shell, of middle ocean,
Amethyst-blue, or a blue of buddleia
Flowers, but shining, or rather
A blue of bluebells, those glittering
Land-of-ocean flowers, now
Empty, empty, floating.

Now wind-driven, snatched by currents,
Bobbing on nearer waves, then wavelets.
Then left, let us say, high
Up a Connemara strand,
Delicate, so delicate
Among stink and sandhoppers,
Where sandpipers ran.

Do You See Your Feet?

Late at night
Before the news,
Feet up, I notice
With surprise
I wear red socks
And saffron shoes.

I see the green
Sides of a book
And white of walls:
I put down
Barnabooth,
And look
At bourgeois Bonnard's
Puzzled face,
And think
I also merge
My room's disorder
Into grace.

My space-heater
Quietly turns,
Noisily light
Twinkles from
Two polished urns,
Yet these red socks,
These saffron shoes,
Prove my bright
Items in the news.

After a Biography

I never saw them as I see them now.
Two tiny lovers in a single bed,
I thought him plump and common,
I thought her poems fey,
Two authentic products
Of an execrable day,
Happily long gone, long dead.

And yet —
Two tiny lovers in a single bed.

After a Death, Agreed

Vague-edged a sun shone whitely through
Our smudging dampness of grey air,
He floated in that blue, that warmth
Which does not reach us here,
And he enlivened all, you say,
By his profound despair.

Châteaubriand on Le Grand Bey

What games — on wet sands, by stakes,
Into shadow and out, what long-shadowed
Games. What hootings through cupped hands
(Being owls), under sea battlements.
Sands, sands, gleaming, being swallowed
By still warm advance of dark.
Being, yes, a Chief, leading, scalping.

It's you. Last home
(At that stake we call Rome).

Tomorrow then, at low tide
Again.

    That was his life, that fancy, those
Games. And in his will — after "the real
Thing" (they say), after power, exile,
Being destitute, return, grandeur, fame,
Folly, pride of imagining (in
Prose), pain — to lie grandiosely
Unnamed, where thrift is, and shit and lift
Of gulls, under huge blocks of wind-dividing
Stone, to know not a thing, to have become
Such ignorant bones. So to remain.
Extinguished. Nothing. Again.

St.-Malo

Jeux Sans Frontières

Under the greenwood tree
In this municipal park we see
How life to-day is happy and free
All under the greenwood tree,
Under the greenwood tree.

Flush from fiddling, our Lady Mayor
Is purring along in the old black Rolls,
To open our summer season of bowls,
Under the greenwood tree.

Along this bench we out-of-works
Finger the 3-d tits — what fun! —
That the ghastly Digger prints in *The Sun*
All under the greenwood tree.

Down by our lake the wild ducks quack.
They are no longer wild, but
Abnormally fat
Under the greenwood tree.

And this stall sells hot dogs and tea.
Pencils as well are provided free
For writing our messages where we pee,
Under the greenwood tree.

And in that paddock reserved for love
By the cuttings shed young Shirley and Ted
Are double-backing as if in bed
Under the greenwood tree.

And in that paddock reserved for dogs
Peke and Dobermann scratch their fleas
After defecating wherever they please,
Under the greenwood tree,
All under the greenwood tree.

History is Changed

Pissarro returns.
Showy white clouds this morning of frost
Are caught in a netting of unleaved
Trees. Released sun drives grey from green.
This lawn might open. Unrecognized,
Unknown, one greater than ever might
Drive by in his car. To-day fifty wafery
Coins of Empress Matilda are found
A foot down on a mountain in Wales,
And history is changed. A gold
Feather falls from the crest of our
Smallest bird. It is on the cards there could
Be some birth. Always there are possibilities
To be thought up on this obovate
Accidental earth.

Six Poems from the German of Christian Morgenstern

i
The Funnels

A pair of funnels stroll by night. They both
  collect inside themselves the white moon-
    light, so clear, so calm, so bright,
     which then descends the runnels
      of these funnels, making
       their woodland way
        much brighter
         und so
          weit-
           er.

ii
Philosophy is Born

The moorland sheep is frightened and amazed
At seeing me. What can this mean?
It means I might be the first man this sheep has ever seen.
An infectious gaze, we stand and stare as if we were asleep.
I might in fact be seeing my first sheep.

iii
Korf's Clock

Two pairs of hands go round
on a clock Korf's made
to indicate time advancing
and time retrograde.

Ten and two it says at once,
it says both three and nine,
and everyone who looks at it
loses his fear of time,

for on this Janus-clock
of Korf's ingenious design
time (as Korf intended)
neutralizes time.

iv
The Moonsheep

The Moonsheep on the wide plain stands.
He waits for the Great Shearer's hands.
           The Moonsheep.

The Moonsheep nibbles a rhizome,
And goes back to his alpine home.
           The Moonsheep.

The Moonsheep in a dream says he
Is Space's dark Infinity.
           The Moonsheep.

The Moonsheep in the dawn lies dead.
His body's white, the sun is red.
           The Moonsheep.

v
The Salmon

To Switzerland, right up the Rhine,
A Salmon swam.

He managed one by one each
Salmon-dam.

Up, up he went to God knows where,
And there,

Twelve feet or more above him, rose
A weir.

Ten feet he jumped so well, and fell.
Dismayed,

Below that Alp three
Weeks he stayed,

And then turned round, at last,
And swam,

In silence, back to Amst-
—Erdam.

        vi
On the Planet of Flies

On the Planet of Flies
it's a poor show for men.
What they do here to flies
flies there do to them.

Men find themselves sticking
on man-papers there,
or swim round and sink
in sugar and beer.

On some points I give
the prize to the flies,
we're not mistakenly swallowed,
or cooked in their pies.

Foreign Travel

A Daring Journey by a Man of Letters Along the Loire from Source to Mouth or Thereabouts in 1912

He took a night express, first class,
From Nantes to Paris, and at last
A seat was soft below his arse,
So long ago, so long ago.

The Loire'd been small and slow and fast,
The Loire'd been wide and also narrow,
And full of sand and very shallow,
So long ago, so long ago.

He'd found the French ate spitted sparrow,
As well as long hind legs of frogs,
And little carts were pulled by dogs,
So long ago, so long ago.

Inns had bad beds and smelly bogs,
And wine the whole way down the Loire
Had been too often weak and sour,
So long ago, so long ago.

Pas autre chose, hélas, à boire,
And *tout droit* hadn't meant turn right,
And he'd been bitten day and night,
So long ago, so long ago.

And flies buzzed black around the tripe
On butchers' stalls down shitty alleys,
And thorns blocked off most tempting valleys,
So long ago, so long ago.

Bored with endless silver sallies
From pointed Gerbier de Jonc
Most of the flow to distant Nantes,
So long ago, so long ago,

He'd thought that what these Frenchmen want
Is fewer Joans of Arc in plaster,
And fewer memories of disaster
So long ago, so long ago,

And trains that travel rather faster.
Nantes, Paris, Calais, Dover,
His venture now is safely over,
Long ago, so long ago.

Nantes, Paris, Calais, Dover,
Now at last he's back at rest
Where every single thing is best,
And even navvies wear a vest,
Long, long ago, so long ago.

In Exile

"They say it is spring, but I do not notice
If tail-upping blackbirds titter
Across my grey-frosted lawns.

They say it is summer, but I have no
Reason for rising. I sleep — and no,
I never see dawns.

They say autumn has gone, and I treat
Forenoons and noons, and luncheons,
And liquor, with nothing but yawns.

And in my winter chess games with our Vicar
I've only a knight with no head to defend me
From all of his pawns."

The Return

So you were still alive.
So, could we have heard them,
Guns thumped on the other side.
So you were pallid as you passed
The laurels and walked up the drive.

So you were bitter, I too young,
Not to feel, but to realize.
So there was no gas in your lung,
So shrapnel yet had to cut you. So
We had everything, everything wrong.

So mud was on you that day.
So it was as if loved wheelbarrow
Paths led not to love, but
Out of love away and away, or were
Barred. So we had trite things only to say.

And you could not stay,
And you went back next day.

Cluck and Crow

Hens' eggs, it becomes appropriate to say,
Are laid by hens, females of an avian
Species. Seldom do we hear now a clucking
Of a hen contentedly delivered of an egg.

Seldom does that which heretofore was called
A clarion, curl from bright males of this
Avian species, on glittering mornings, from run
To run, stackyard to stackyard. Yolks are pale.

I could round these stanzas by complaining —
But this concern permits us not be more obvious
Than it requires — that capital has driven
Hens into cages, and hens' eggs into rigid soft

Containers. With tigers, hens lived free in Upper
Burmese jungles. Hens flew west. And Greeks carved
Hens on temple pediments. By hens' bones Greeks
Told their future, eating of course hens' flesh,

Hens' eggs as well, procuring — et cetera, et cetera —
Softness with hens' feathers too. But let us not
Be hypocrites. Were not old ex-egg-layers
Boiled? As the child said of the pallid

Old bird generously hidden in striped onion
And white sauce, on the mahogany table,
In front of guests, with the best crested silver
Out, "Is that the old black hen?"

Outside His Verandah

Behind Passion Flowers — which last is it till lunch time, or
    an hour? —
His young girl is typing for him, tat-a-tat, a-tat, a-tat,
And if another young rat crosses the *tole plastique* above her,
His young girl will scream, then tat-a-tat, tat-a-tat confidently
Resume. He lies back, he re-enters a lost day when to-day
Would have seemed — bad or good — a most enviable dream.

He thinks of that homo novelist, his friend —
Of how he was lonely, how he was afraid;
And how behind a foreign locked door came his end.
He thinks it will be time soon for drinks,
And the tat-a-tat stops, with "You should move into the
    shade."
He as well is lonelier than I supposed, and is afraid.

Night with Mist

Between trunks of oak a sky of night
Meets a black earth on which no house
Or car lights shine. All that I feel is stirring
Of a colder air. Rustling of a high stream
Is nearly all I hear.

This is true night, though thin mist greys
The sky and lets only a group or two of stars
Shine through, and I am not much conscious either
Of myself or you. Grass — perhaps grass grows
More heavy with mid-October dew.

Mushrooms, for sure, push up black earth,
Veiled, and intact as long as crawlers sleep.
Earwigs have crowded into hollow stems
And now perhaps floats by a soundless owl.
So it may be that I

Like that soft hunting bird, experiencing — for
Once — true night, for once am fitted
To aboriginal circumstance in this long
Restful night — to the first nature of my scarcely
Thinking animal life.

Atavism — though it cannot last. Throw-back
To a continuum of unexpecting life. No calendar,
No clock. No sense of more than
Instant time. Knowing alone — for now — cool
Reverberations of a perfect rhyme.

Again and Again

You remember — as near as you could to moaning men —
The crack on stone edges of hard truncheons
Which had missed head, shoulders, arms?
Yes, I remember them.

You remember horses, reined by cold disciplined men,
That plunged on rolled marbles and ball-bearings,
Pipes skirling, screams, flocked starling men?
I remember them.

You remember breaks, booing, scattering, returning,
Another charge, scattering again, now an old shame
Evaporated with time comes back again?
Yes, I remember them.

Will you remember how water-cannon and TV crews
Advance, how tear-gas sneaks into alleys, this opening
Movement to growling music of an odious dance? Yes,
I shall remember them.

Peace be unto you. These black heaps lightly skinned
With trees cover an unextinguished heat of being
Abused and losing hope. Stones there lie ready,

And again and again we shall have reason
To remember them.

No Trouble

Socialism, like the Sermon on the Mount,
The Tories say is much too difficult for men. So then?
Since Toryism, torture, hatred, greed, come
Easily to men, let's plump for them.

Heart Failure

How he would have enjoyed (leaning
Back, like an advert, lighting his pipe)
The suddenness, waders on, five minutes
Before, of his exit from life,

Knowing how pissed his relations would be
At the way he had spent his own wealth,
And certain that Life, in a new bra,
Would be upstairs admiring herself.

Ruskin's View, Kirby Lonsdale

So this is Mr Ruskin's View,
This ultimacy of green;
Benched beyond graves, I see
What Ruskin and Co. mean.

A river draws a curve: parked
Meadows are marvellously wide;
And green shelves up, then back into wild
Fells on the far side.

It is October: trees not — or
It seems so — too intentionally set
In order and disorder, display
No dead tones yet.

I see past graves what that
Besotted aesthete and the others mean —
A peace-be-unto-us, in cool
Matt affinities of green.

Sick Priest

He lay in his bed as close as could be
To that womb he had been denied,
And reviewing his intimate being
He was not at all satisfied.

Picnics, yes, on a pollard tree;
Then with a near-nude girl alongside,
A sweet stink of seaweed and a kettle boiling
And how, after, both of them cried.

There was "Do this in memory of me",
There was God would be his sure guide,
And by God how that sure God's guiding
Had shunted him to one side.

Time for his two croissants and tea.
It was warmth's nook he had been denied.
Better for him if he stopped persisting,
If he gobbled his croissants, and died.

Cleric on the Air

Cleric on the air says
I am, like you, of our time.

When mystery is mentioned
I am aware there is nothing to it.

So what on earth do I mean when I affirm
It is God (or the Deity, should I say?)

Who feeds us with most desirable
Vitamins or intimations of mystery?

Of course — and I am always jolly
About this — I do believe in the Deity.

He is not mysterious, he is a Fact.
I am of our time, like you I respond

To the mystery of e.g. wild flowers (pick not)
And of music (from disc),

And you call me (since on the air
I have mastered lying and laughing

Simultaneously) a bleeding
Hypocrite.

A Broken Wheel

Into a brief unevenness of grass
Purpled by Judas flowers, a bridge of stone
Raises a rough way across a dark-down stream.
That rough way mounts, loose, though one side's
Walled, by zigzags, through inked ilex scrub,

Up, up to a camel's hump of *château* stone,
Abandoned, centuries unroofed, unbeamed,
President on a profitless domain.
They rebuilt by this broken bridge, beside
Their seigneurial mill (that broken wheel).

There's the lean seigneur, slicing *saumon fumé*
For his hotel guests. That's his wife, that long-
Footed, light dressed, slightly stumbling
Lady Ottoline. I will not analyse these
Extra guests she welcomes awkwardly, shop

People from the near town the seigneurs owned.
Now tourists are enough for both — why not?
No lazy wheel, or it seems so, now turns.
Across this wide once hunters' hearth a long
Swart log of ilex sullenly burns.

Idyll in a Victorian Vicarage

He comforted those bereft by wreck,
She gave them soup and flannel.
He watched the red-legged choughs
Along his dangerous cliffs,
And lifting terns; she filled
Her Wardian case with ferns.
Death made him think of death
In a calm vicarage in North Devon,
And made him draw the pair of them,
Cheerily, by God's express permission,
Effing as they flew to Heaven.

Clovelly

A Visit to the Ledger Stones of Clerical Ancestors

It does not much upset me
To know so little of those who
Bequeathed me my name.

I suppose they were kindly, I see
They were locals, who never
Whored much after fame.

They took their degrees,
They returned to their acres,
And accepted mildly what came.

They knew sweetness and bitter,
A spray of olive on stone
Above a child's name.

They were buried in sunshine and frost
Who were conceived
In the warmth and the rain.

God's peace they had promised
Their people, which their descendant also
Would welcome, supposing it came.

S.F.

Defiant simple Nemo I do understand
But not this loony band. Through a vast
Vertigo of vacancy inside them their ships
Whizz. These ships they people with cold
Crews. These cold crews wear curving uniforms.
These cold crews must be for ever young. These
Cold crews lack tackle to mate or masturbate.
These cold curved crews push from the heart-strand.

   Sad simple subaqueous Nemo, that wandering man,
Was all the same attached to the land.

Smooth Accident

I am letting my head descend
Through my combing hands,
I am making a noise the sea
Makes, coming back over the sands.
I scent the scent of the pines
Crossing the dunes to these sands
And meeting this scent of the sea,
Of these salty sands. If I open
My eyes — how delicate webs of birds
Will be printing the sands. I shall
See the gleam sink in, I shall see
That gleam come back to the sands.

Peace.

I am letting my head descend
Through my combing hands.

Return to England

Black, heavy, green, too green, our now recovered
Scene. Tunnels below trees. Everywhere there might
Be moss-soft statues, yet of whom? We have no
Gods — can no more than pretend? But in pretence

Or recollection, in imagining, is possible good.
I imagine sylvans in our wood. Beyond
I crown a goddess of young springing corn
With flowers of June. Now are no Giverny poppies

Or best-blue flowers of the corn. A coach marked
Supreme Travel passes my window; and no such
Travel will take me now to wide fields as
Heretofore of scarlet and of blue; and udders

Are no longer swished by lanky buttercups
In Agricultural College meads. It's not
God's sentiment to regret these ancient colours
Which were, on unacknowledged balance, of high

Good to men. I set up my — not memorial because
We have them still — no, my tribute to
The increasing greed of educated farmers
And their spruce accountancy. To them,

Returned, I dedicate, in clouded June, this
Heavy blackish monotone of the prose of green,
All of it, after all, fat with profit, and obscene.

A Relic

Love came out of the sea
In a pink and savage place,
And before anyone of our race
Caught the sound of her voice
Or a glimpse of her face,
Handmaidens swept her away
In the silver cloud Rolls-Royce.

All the same,
A scent then haunted the air,
Rose No.1 and a small
Shore lily flowered immediately there,
And the sun of that dawning glittered
On a fallen,
Blonde pubic hair.

Over the Hills

Over the hills and far away
Is being here and never there,
Whatever the flash advertisements say
About over the hills and far away.

Over the hills and far away
Is no wild rose on the blue of Wales:
It is always where we remain to-day,
Whatever these flashing adverts say.

Some still imagine Holy Grails
Over the hills and far away
And continue kneeling at altar-rails,
Awaiting that signal which always fails.

It is always here and never there,
Whatever the flash advertisements say.
Lack of hope and tinge of fear,
This haversack is heavy to wear

On the way to the kiss which is never given,
Though we do not move a mile from here,
Driving ourselves, or else being driven,
To a field of snow on a hill of heaven.

The Pairs

Appalling that breath and death should be a pair.
There are pairs which fix a squalid atmosphere.

Again, knife and life, hell and tolling of a bell,
Beauty and do your duty.

Such pairs do, in some degree, belong to now dead years.
In mercy I am mainly for regret, and then forget.

How Is It?

How is it, when those alone
With imaginary sparse beards, those
Antique atavists, those short of intellect
And breath, go on believing now
They will be living
After death?

How is it, when we know our marvellous
Mechanism without pulse of blood breaks
In decay, though orientated by the toes
To an impossible
Resurrection Day?

How is it, when we know there will be
No future hunting, no need for real or token
Steeds in our graves, Château d'Yquem in beakers,
Or clay
Female slaves?

How is it then, that past the obit in *The Times*
Among the cemetery lines we bend,
Read, revere, not living, but
That invisible husk which now is no
More than
Calcium and dust?

Chicory-Eyed Author

He was only a little man,
Not even as tall as you,
A rubbery ball of a little man
Whose eyes, between edges of white,
Were excessively blue.

Go on, ring the bell of his house,
Which now belongs to the state,
Pay at the door, and being small
Yourself, you will learn
A few ways to compensate.

On the ground floor the seigneur
Sat down at this polished oak:
It was rather too bad that puffs of wind
Down this seigneurial chimney blurred
His Middle Ages with smoke.

When it cleared, he bounced
Up these wide stairs to his mosque.
It was here he unbuttoned his shoes
And revealed his odorous
Striped cotton socks.

It was here he called "Allah is One",
And knocked his brow on the floor,
Until thoughts about death, and that
Catafalque there, made him
Skip to delights next door.

Next door among daggers and divans
He knocked back cup after cup
Of sherbet (or calva or cognac)
Which a naked Circassian, he thought,
Came in to fill up.

That point finished his fancy — no doubt
A lack of cash was the cause.
He would blow out his tallow behind
Coloured glass, and sneak
From his fancied amours

To this room dusty with whitewash,
To this actual mattress of hay.
By the way, lift that lid on the table:
In plaster, that is the Hand of the Master,
Which time has turned grey.

It was here he was cornered by dying,
And cut to his tiny size.
Even so, death failed to extinguish,
The carpenter saw with surprise, that
Chicory-blue of his eyes.

Without Regret

Work without regret for lacking fame.
Work without putting c for copyright
In a small circle at the foot of your
Photo or your name. Famous, infamous,
Unnoticed, it will be all the same.

Four Poems about Poetry
i
Poetry

Poetry is always in a bad way
And has been since its first day,
And will be so at the end of time,
So mop your eyes for Metre, Rhythm and Rhyme.

ii
The Difficult Poems

The difficult poems are the ones in which
Like Fox Talbot perfecting his Pencil of Nature
You try fixations of brief insubstantial intimations.

They are not brilliant as a river, solemn as a hill,
They occur, in no particular situation, no special season.
        Without visible reason
        They unify, they underlie.

iii
Transference

Writing against Russia pays.
I knew a poetaster who did it — in prose.
He had a Soviet wife in his young days.
She left him, and thorns choked the rose.

iv
The Offering

Must the dove be sacrificed?
Must its feathers be dribbled with blood
From its nostrils and mouth?
Must the dove be burnt?
There are bad things to be learnt.

Advice to a Half-Hatched Poet

Blades, that bloody Northern Knife,
Loutish Leakey soiling life,
Chirping Cheadle all these years
Have caused an earache in your ears?

My lad, pipe down, I say pipe down:
Respect the simper of the town,
Make it clear your versing follows
The versing of these scabbed Apollos.

OR — Mildred will not speak for you
And Haystack will not squeak for you:
It will be up the creek for you
And royalties will not peak for you.

   It will be sneers, lad,
   Week by week for you.

Sentimental Error Among Ruins

These lanes were paved:
Monks pattered here
On yellow stones
Who are now bones.

But don't complain
Of how since then
Graces and disgraces
Have changed places —

As if nothing base is
Ever to be seen in
Holy places —
Ditto, faces.

With It

What is the essence of *It*
That all of us need to be *With*?
Like cocaine to brown Coca-Cola
It relates to *It*'s obvious rhyme:
Merde à la vanille, said Zola;
Which is *It* most of the time.

The Floods

They made a deity of this enormous river,
Flowing evenly, azure, and wide.
They knew that deities cannot be defied,
Though, with luck, and gift, they can be gratified.
At times this deity crossed her banks of sand,
Cavorted through willows, swept away
Worshippers and flocks, ruined their plats of land,
Then — grace to her — so satisfied, sank,
And flowed evenly, and blue, and wide.

Châteauneuf-sur-Loire

Water-Mill of Love

If you say Love is the intent,
The He and She of it
The necessary accident,
I must ask whose intent
And, acknowledging the need
Of generation and descent,

Admit that He and She and Love
Must equally have come by accident:
In bodies only can these three exist:
The grain's fed in
And under the revolving stone
Out comes the grist.

Antic

With a shrug and a sotto "I'm sorry",
Death to be sure takes off
All who are good and true.

But — pin on his medals
And orders — he
Takes off the others too.

Atavists

That satellite, that slow speck of not at all
Angelic light, orbits a quiet mauve
Of midsummer night up there.

And down here that old, old, all
Skin-and-bone White monk no doubt has by now
Doddered to sleep in his chair.

To-morrow, when day reaches eleven, we shall be
Admitted and permitted to share archaic
Beauties of Benedictine prayer.

We shall wait, with a congregation of up-ended
Stone coffins, which were cut, and filled,
Heretofore, in God alone knows what year.

Ligugé

Drunken Drivers See the Sights at Whitsun

Three elderly abbots occasioned these bones
Which should one day re-knit (to angelic applause).
But I see there are not enough legs for all three,
And how will they plead without jaws?

Through that hole in the floor these old birds
Were let down to their temporary tomb,
And angels are carved on the rock *là-haut*
To entice them at last from their gloom

To face Judge and Devil and be shown into Heaven
Or likelier chucked into Hell,
To be braised there for ever, and buggered
By hot-dildoed demons as well.

Now for two francs a head you've stared at these dead
And to-night your holiday Whitsun ends,
So drive off with care round your very steep bends or
Be dead as an abbot, my drunken friends,
Quite as dead as an abbot, my friends.

St.-Emilion

Satellite

What's next after soiling the moon
And breaking its antique tune?

A vicious satellite
Transects to-night,

Acolyte of Red Mars
And this flower-field of stars.

And from its doorway our race,
Like a fool, stares into space

As if no night sounds floated here,
Trembling and clear,

As if our earth-grace
Were not enough for our case.

Battlefield

Swords clash across the open
On this large scale map
Where harvest fields are
Hedgeless ochre and, again,
  The corn-golds are in flower.

Kings' blood fouled this warm
Ochre centuries back.
Came later piddling strife of pike-armed
Rebel and dissenter, indifferent also
  To that sweet weed's flower,

Where holiday cars swish through, stop
Briefly to fill up; one turning, parking
For a late sun picnic on this
Acre, on which the not
  Regarded corn-golds flower.

The kids play rounders, parents
Snatch a nap. Among these legatees
Has History no conscious taker
For whom these most loquacious
  Corn-weeds flower.

Time. Bottles, paper plates, the one-
Year-old's plastic cup are packed.
They leave, crossing this dry patch
Of the dead king-maker, crushing these
  Late golds in flower.

They're home. The resentful pusscat
Stalks from lap to lap. Cheerfully again
They live and work, light-years from the
Sere acre of these obstinate unheeded weeds
  Of history in flower.

Swans and Beetles

Would it be any good keeping them on at school,
Or introducing them for life's sake
To wild swans between icebergs on a lake,
When they prefer the little agilities
Of water-boatmen over a pool?

The Widow

On her broken whirligig stool, on folds
Of old curtains, alone,
She will play most of to-day
Bach, Haydn and Mendelssohn.

The damp old wind of the Greeks
Curls up from Valéry's sea,
Which is not always blue, alas.
Rain drips from her black pine tree.

Thunder again. More rain
Roars down from the gutters.
Pink garlics bend outside. A crack,
And the one bulb flutters.

This much is certain now,
She hears no thunder, no phone.
On her old curtains, alone, she plays
Bach, Haydn and Mendelssohn.

Dubious Marriage

Whether they copulated it's not possible to say.
It seems he only loved women three feet away.
It seems he could not bear a human touch upon his skin,
His tragedy to be outside and never in.
No one-with-one was ever one for him.

The Wicked Poet

There should have been some to-day's
Medico of high degree to help him
Through the palpable heavy air
Which impeded him always, everywhere?

Where was the ease, the ease? Not on
His knees. Not down the next street.
To-morrow and the next street came,
And it was all the same.

Out sparkled sunlight after rain
And rain, and gobbets of rotten meat,
Dog shit, and human piddle
Spread from the foaming kennel.

Inside, he was — well, we cannot tell.
Outside, as ever supercilious, and dressed
So smartly, and so vain.
And still, although he wrote, the pain,

The pain. His rapier flashed, the dull
Cully — I use the verb they used — was
Properly and contemptuously slain.
No good in that. Still the unstaunched pain.

So he rhymed on, and swore, and drank
And swanked, then stepped from duchess
And ridotto down the stinking lane
To the cerused breasts

Of Mother Redcap's girls again.

The Cornish Dancer

They pranced him round Porthallow Green,
They flew him on to Seaton Sand.
The tide was out. There was a red full moon.

Further they flew, to the King's cellar at Versailles.
They scoffed his wine. He stole a golden bowl.
Back home they flew. And it's a coarse canard

To say he sold that bowl to goldsmith Huddy
In Liskeard. All we know about that precious bowl
Is that he never showed it to a soul.

Saint in the Summer Rain

Though I am not saint, and never was monk or abbot,
I was moved that this neat saintly skull
In the Norman church cupboard bore one of the two
Names I am known by. His skull was best of the skulls inside
And we looked a long time at each other, the blue-grey
(As my passport particulars say) and the hollow eyed.
And I remembered to do what the notice said, which was
"Switch off the light in the cupboard, please,
When you go outside."

Outside it was raining like hell, and our car
Didn't start too well, and I thought, Extend any line, and sooner
Or later, further or near, you'll come to some genuine
Grim human hell. And as I drove off I remarked to my
Namesake, "Well, for your head and the rest of you under
The grass hereabouts in your bed it can't be after all too bad
To be boxed in the null
Preposterous calm of the dead."

A Vision

Everything ordinary is transfigured suddenly,
As if a shining deity invisible to me
Casually has made shapes, colours, objects here
One in a melody,

Which is played to me as long as I stare,
Which I play as long as I dare,
Which I break, so that
It will not betray me here.

Thank You

What's the good of mourning
This passing of poets?
Be glad they have lived,

Intermittently sozzled with words,
Unslurred, on this side and that side
Of the Absurd.

If I Could Suppose

If I could suppose
You existed, a
Tender swaying Goddess
Of Forgiveness,

I would pray
Forgive me now
My timidities
And my indifferences.

Forgive me these
Above other offences
I have been cheerful with,
Inside my white defences.

Sedum acre Linn.

For us all it's so;
Only rooms of our first consciousness
We intimately know;
Outside, only that arch of brick
Through which the fancy stairs
Upward to somewhere go —

Only on that lichen-plattered wall
Long yellow beards
Of that strange flower
Which by its Latin name
Alone, no longer
Knowing it, we know.

Exiled, before we sleep
In half-sleep we return;
But in that now fading room
Only to cold ashes can
That scarlet, secret, magic cave
Inside our dark coals burn.

It must be so,
I say, my younger love, to you,
Dismayed, yet not dismayed,
Afraid, yet by you less afraid,
I knew all this was so,
My love, so long ago.

Shaving

Heat of the hot water runs through the cold.
It's the other way round with the old,
Who can seldom quite turn off the cold.

Emeritus

The soft silk ashes of Emeritus
They've emptied on Tom Tiddler's Ground,
Only his books remain, unread,
Unreadable, and unrenowned.

New Year's Eve

What does it mean, this brown owl's
Feather scotch-taped to the bathroom shelf?
I do not ask myself, Will it be there
For six months of another year?

Become Old

If you reach high age and then lean back
And press your eyebrows and reflect,
You know you can't with pleasure
Have much unexpected to expect.

And it's no substitute to recollect.

On a Sentimental Charlatan

The unctuosity of his fart
Proclaims the load of shit
Concealed below his heart.

At the Lectern

Hear how the First Lesson endeth.
It was when we dropped the 3rd. person singular
Ending in —eth that we began thinking more
About life than death.

The Fresh One

Is it possible she came from the land?
It is only possible she came from the sea
And imprinted the sand where
The new flowers began.
It is only possible she came from the sea
And not from the land.

Tolling the Same

Though in life as if demented
New modes of killing and
Of dying are invented,

Being dead remains the same:
All death is known, all death
Retains that single name,

And as well we grimly know
It spits into the eyes of love,
However quietly we go.

All Square

(Ungratefully)

If bloody surgeons need a bloody cut
To make them bloody pee,
It shows that life for bloody surgeons
Is the same as life for bloody me.